D1707951

FamilyFitCooking

Easy, filling, never-boring, healthy, fun recipes the whole family will enjoy!

Nicole Phillips

This book is dedicated to my husband, who is my best friend and has supported me in the kitchen for years. Some of the most unforgettable experiences happen there or around the dining-room table.

One of our first memories as a couple was throwing spaghetti against the wall in college to see whether it was fully cooked.

THANK YOU NOTES

I would like to start this book by thanking God for the guidance He gave me on this new journey, paving the way for this book to be written. I am thankful beyond words for Him aligning my passion with talent to allow me to cook healthy and delicious foods—and then giving me the opportunity to put my ideas into a book to help others eat well and learn to enjoy nourishing their bodies. I also thank my amazing husband, Paul, for his encouragement and support, for his cooking skills, and for coming up with many of the recipes with me. I thank my three beautiful babies, Madalyn Diane (11), Jaxon Ryan (10), and Miss Layla Rae (8) for always trying my new concoctions and for supporting and encouraging me even at their young ages. Next, I thank my sister, Jade Scott, for encouraging me to start writing and sharing recipes on a bigger level and for supporting me along the way. Last but not least, I thank my mom and dad, Julia and Philip Keeler, for raising me to know God and seek His will for my life and my baby sister, Tori Bruner, for walking alongside me as I continue to grow to know God better. This is one of my wildest dreams!

CONTENTS

INTRODUCTION

HELLO! I'm Nicole, and I am a total foodie, but . . . I also love everything health and fitness related. I LOVE to eat healthily but not feel deprived. I have learned to incorporate FUN and DELICIOUS recipes that are EASY to make and are healthy too! Healthy DOES NOT have to be boring! I am a mom of three, wife of a firefighter, and part-time teacher of students with autism . . . life gets BUSY, and I totally get that! That does not mean your nutrition has to suffer or that you have to eat bland and boring foods. I decided to write this cookbook for all the busy families out there who still want to eat delicious and healthy meals around the table together—or let's be honest, who eat on the go (or in shifts) most nights! I also wrote this cookbook for all the moms and dads (and college kids, and single men and women who work long hours—for everyone, really) who think eating healthily during the day is not possible . . . IT IS, and it is TASTY! Please do not be intimidated by any of these recipes, prep/cook times, or ingredients . . . every one of you can TOTALLY make ALL of them!

I also want to encourage you to be adventurous with your food, try new things, mix different ingredients, and make it work! I came up with many of these recipes by taking the healthy factor of what my family was eating most days to the next level. You can totally make what your family is eating into a healthier version, cut the unhealthy carbs and add healthy ones, and ADD MORE VEGGIES!

Also, tweak these recipes until they are perfect for you! That is how I came up with so many of my ideas . . . taking a recipe and tweaking it until my family and I love it. You should enjoy nutritious food that feeds your body well!

One more thing—ladies, especially, DO NOT BE AFRAID TO GRILL! It is life changing!! So easy and no cleanup!!

I should also mention that I prefer Himalayan salt (it is natural and has a ton of minerals). Therefore, almost all my recipes call for it, but you do not have to use it for them to turn out delicious!

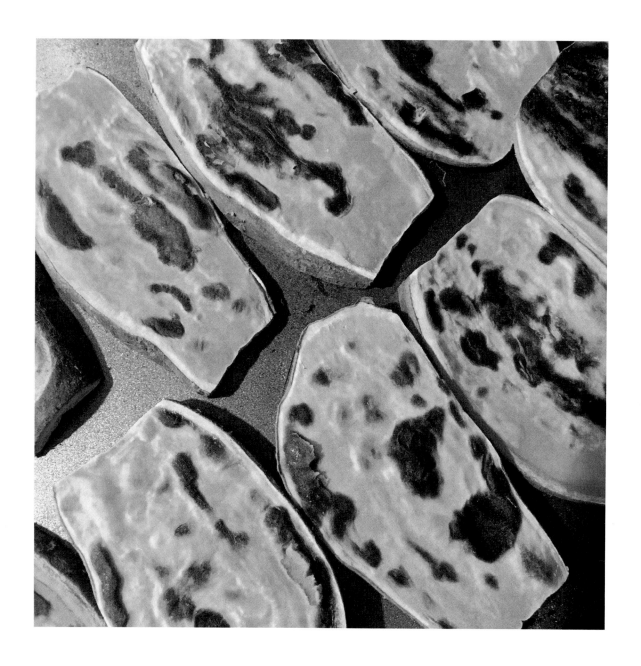

1
FOOD PREP TIPS

It is ALWAYS helpful to have healthy options on hand! Here are some of my food prep staples that will help you make healthy choices on a busy day AND will be helpful when making many of the recipes in this book. They are super easy to fit into a busy routine.

SWEET POTATO/POTATO TOAST

The options are endless with sweet potato/potato toast!
SERVINGS: as many as you want to prep/2 slices = 1 serving of carbs
PREP TIME: 5 minutes
COOK TIME: 30 minutes

INGREDIENTS:

Sweet potatoes and/or potatoes (as many as you want for the week; each potato makes at least 4 slices).

PREPARATION:

1. Preheat your oven to 400 degrees.
2. Cut your potato lengthwise using a big knife or mandoline to create slices that are about ¼-inch thick.
3. Arrange the slices on a wire rack set on a large baking sheet.
4. Bake for 30 minutes or until potatoes are tender and a little crispy. You can rotate the pan and flip each piece halfway through if you want (see how they are looking in your oven), but it is not necessary.
5. Remove the pan from the oven and allow the slices to cool completely before storing them in a container in the fridge (it's important that you allow them to cool before stacking them in the container, or they will get sweaty and take longer to toast when you're ready to eat).
6. When it's go time, simply add the desired number of slices to the toaster or toaster oven and toast away. I set my toaster to medium/high, and it takes only one toasting cycle to get them how I like them (warm, bubbly, and crispy on the edges). Yours may need more or less time, depending on your toaster.

TURKEY BACON

**Dirty little secret . . . I BAKE my bacon! This way, it takes only 2 minutes of prep time, and there is NO CLEANUP!

**I highly recommend preparing bacon for the week . . . everything is better with bacon!

SERVINGS: as much as you want to prep/4 slices = 1 serving of protein

PREP TIME: 2 minutes

COOK TIME: 20 minutes

INGREDIENTS:

Turkey bacon

PREPARATION:

1. Line a cookie sheet with foil.
2. Lay bacon in a single layer on the cookie sheet.
3. Put the bacon in a cold oven.
4. Set the oven to 375 degrees.
5. Bake for 20–25 minutes or until they reach your desired crispiness . . . I like mine CRISP!

SHREDDED CROCKPOT CHICKEN

SERVINGS: 4

PREP TIME: 5 minutes

COOK TIME: 3–4 hours (but you just leave it and forget about it)

INGREDIENTS:

1 pound of boneless, skinless chicken breasts or thighs (depending on what you want prepped for the week).

I use 2 hearty dashes of one of the following . . .

- BBQ sauce (with dark or white meat)
- salsa verde (white meat)
- Tessemae's lemon garlic salad dressing (white meat)

**See chapter 12 for the exact products I use.

PREPARATION:

1. Put the chicken in the crockpot.
2. Add your sauce/salsa/dressing.
3. Set the crockpot to low and cook for 3–4 hours (until chicken can be shredded with a fork, don't overcook or the chicken will be dry).
4. Shred the chicken.
5. For BBQ sauce only, strain and discard the juices from chicken, put the chicken back in the crockpot, add a few more dashes of sauce. For salsa and salad dressing, straining is not necessary, you could add a little splash of dressing/salsa (totally personal preference).
6. VOILA! Chicken is prepped for recipes for the week!

HARD-BOILED EGGS

SERVINGS: as many eggs as you want/2 eggs = 1 serving of protein

PREPTIME: 2 minutes

COOK TIME: 3-5 minutes

INGREDIENTS:

Eggs

PREPARATION:

I love making my hard-boiled eggs in the pressure cooker! Simply follow the directions for your specific cooker (here is what I do...add one cup of water to the pressure pot, add eggs, close the lid, cook on low heat for 3 minutes, when time is up, remove lid and eggs from pressure pot, chill eggs in cold water and ice, when eggs are cool, peel) . My pressure cooker takes 3 minutes of actual cook time. The shells FALL RIGHT OFF!

ROASTED VEGGIES

**This is so simple without any cleanup!!! Just coat some veggies in olive oil, sprinkle them with salt and pepper, throw them in the oven, set the timer, and go about your business. When the timer goes off, take the veggies out, let them cool, put them in Tupperware, store them in the refrigerator, throw the foil away, and continue to go about your business.

SERVINGS: as many as you want/1 cup = 1 serving
PREP TIME: 5 minutes
COOK TIME: 20–40 minutes

INGREDIENTS:
Whatever veggies you would like to have in the fridge to grab throughout the week. My staples are . . .

- Broccoli
- Cauliflower
- Brussels sprouts
- Asparagus
- Carrots
- Spaghetti squash
- Butternut squash

Olive oil

Himalayan salt

Freshly ground black pepper

**I do not make all these every week—I choose what I'm in the mood for.

PREPARATION:
For all veggies except squash . . .
1. Preheat your oven to 375 degrees.
2. Line a baking sheet with foil.

3. Put the veggies on the baking sheet.
4. Drizzle them with olive oil, and sprinkle them with salt and pepper.
5. Move the veggies around with your hands to get them evenly coated.
6. Bake them for 20 minutes.
7. Let them cool.
8. Put in them Tupperware.
9. Throw them in the refrigerator to have for the week.

For the squash . . .
1. Preheat oven to 400 degrees.
2. Line the baking sheet with foil.
3. Cut spaghetti squash in half lengthwise (do the same for the butternut squash but then cut the halves in half to make quarters).
4. Scoop all the seeds out using a fork.
5. Rub a teaspoon of olive oil, ½ teaspoon salt, and ¼ teaspoon pepper on each piece squash.
6. Place the pieces face down on the baking sheet.
7. Bake them for 40 minutes.

HEALTHY BACON, LETTUCE, TOMATO, and EGG IS IN CHAPTER 3: LUNCHES, BUT I LOVE IT FOR BREAKFAST TOO!

2

BREAKFASTS

Here are some DELICIOUS breakfast recipes, including FRENCH TOAST and PANCAKES!!! I hope you enjoy them as much as I do! I actually prefer the taste of these healthy choices over the unhealthy ones!

EGG MUFFINS

SERVINGS: 6 / 2 muffins per serving
PREP TIME: 10 minutes
COOKING TIME: 20–25 minutes

INGREDIENTS:
Nonstick cooking spray
12 eggs
Himalayan salt
Freshly ground black pepper
¾ cup spiralized butternut squash (you may have a tad left over)
4 slices cooked turkey bacon, chopped (see page 12)
1 cup spinach, chopped

PREPARATION:
1. Preheat your oven to 350 degrees.
2. Spray a cupcake tray with nonstick cooking spray.
3. Crack 12 eggs into a large mixing bowl.
4. Add a desired amount of salt and pepper to the eggs and beat the egg mixture.
5. Divide the butternut squash evenly into each cup on the cupcake tray.
6. Pour the egg mixture on top of the butternut squash in each cup.
7. Divide the turkey bacon evenly and place it on top of the eggs.
8. Divide the spinach evenly and it place on top of the eggs.
9. Bake for 20–25 minutes.

**These refrigerate well and are great to have on hand to grab and heat in the microwave for a few seconds. I food prep them often!
**I also love them because the options are ENDLESS! Change up your veggies, don't add the bacon, do whatever you are in the mood for . . . that's what you do, AND you really can't mess them up!!! You can also do a variety of options at once! #winning

PROTEIN PANCAKES

SERVINGS: 4 / 2 pancakes per serving (8 total pancakes)
PREP TIME: 5 minutes
COOK TIME: 15 minutes

INGREDIENTS:
Nonstick cooking spray

2 super ripe bananas

4 eggs

2 scoops protein powder (I live by Shakeology)

¼ cup unsweetened almond milk

2 healthy dashes cinnamon

½ teaspoon baking powder

½ teaspoon Himalayan salt

PREPARATION:
1. Heat the griddle to medium, and spray it with cooking spray.
2. Blend the bananas, eggs, protein powder, cinnamon, and baking powder (I use my NutriBullet when I cut the recipe in half).
2. Pour the batter onto the griddle (sometimes, I use an ice-cream scooper) to form pancakes.
3. Once they're browned (2–3 minutes) on the bottom, flip them.
4. Brown them on the other side.
5. Serve . . . I like to top mine with a little nut butter and some fresh fruit and/or nuts, followed by a tiny drizzle of pure maple syrup.

HEALTHY OAT PANCAKES

SERVINGS: 4/ 2 pancakes per serving (8 total pancakes)
PREP TIME: 10 minutes
COOK TIME: 15 minutes

INGREDIENTS:
Nonstick cooking spray
1 cup unsweetened vanilla almond milk (or coconut milk)
2 eggs
1 ripe banana
1 teaspoon pure vanilla extract
1 teaspoon baking powder
½ teaspoon ground cinnamon
¼ teaspoon Himalayan salt
2 cups old-fashioned whole-grain rolled oats

PREPARATION:
1. Place the milk, eggs, banana, vanilla, baking powder, cinnamon, salt, and oats in a blender and blend until smooth (when I cut the recipe in half, I use my NutriBullet . . . so easy)!
2. Heat the griddle to medium heat, and spray it with cooking spray.
3. Pour the batter onto the griddle (sometimes, I use an ice-cream scooper) to form pancakes.
4. Once they're browned (2–3 minutes) on the bottom, flip them.
5. Brown them on the other side.
6. Serve . . . I like to top mine with a little nut butter and some fresh fruit, followed by a tiny drizzle of pure maple syrup.

POTATO AVOCADO TOAST

SERVINGS: 1 / 2 slices toast
PREP TIME: 5 minutes
COOK TIME: 2 minutes

INGREDIENTS:
2 slices of sweet potato or potato toast (see page 11)
½ avocado, mashed
2 hard-boiled eggs (see page 14)
2 dashes Himalayan salt
2 sprinkles freshly ground black pepper
2 tablespoons cilantro, chopped
Dash of Everything but the Bagel seasoning (see chapter 12)

PREPARATION:
1. Heat 2 slices of sweet potato toast in the toaster (see page 11).
2. Mash ¼ avocado on each piece of toast.
3. Top the mashed avocado with a dash of Himalayan salt and freshly ground black pepper.
4. Slice the hard-boiled eggs.
5. Top each piece of toast with the egg slices.
6. Top the eggs with cilantro and Everything but the Bagel seasoning.

SWEET POTATO TOAST

SERVINGS: 1 / 2 slices toast
PREP TIME: 5 minutes
COOK TIME: 2 minutes

INGREDIENTS:
2 slices of sweet potato or potato toast (see page 11)
1 tablespoon nut butter of choice (no sugar added)
½ banana, sliced
2 dashes Himalayan salt
2 dashes cinnamon
Nuts of choice (only if desired); just a sprinkle

PREPARATION:
1. Heat 2 slices of sweet potato toast in the toaster (see page 11).
2. Spread ½ tablespoon of nut butter on each slice of toast.
3. Place the banana slices on top of the nut butter.
4. Dash the salt and cinnamon over the top.
5. Sprinkle with nuts, if you choose.
6. ENJOY.

GUILTLESS FRENCH TOAST

SERVINGS: 4 / 1 slice of French toast per serving
PREP TIME: 10 minutes
COOK TIME: 6–8 minutes

INGREDIENTS:

4 eggs
4 tablespoons unsweetened almond milk
1 teaspoon vanilla extract
3 teaspoons pure maple syrup, divided use (cooking and topping)
1 teaspoon ground cinnamon
4 slices sprouted or Ezekiel bread
2 teaspoons ghee

PREPARATION:

1. Combine the eggs, almond milk, vanilla, 1 teaspoon maple syrup, and cinnamon in a large mixing bowl and whisk away.
2. Soak each slice of bread in the mixture for about 3 minutes, turning them halfway through.
3. Heat the ghee on a griddle, turned to medium heat.
4. Add the bread, and cook for 2–3 minutes on each side.
5. Serve . . . I like to top mine with fresh fruit (berries or bananas) and maybe some nuts and then drizzle them with the rest of the syrup.

LEMON POPPYSEED WAFFLES

SERVINGS: 4 / 2 waffles each serving
PREP TIME: 5 minutes
COOK TIME: 15 minutes

INGREDIENTS:
1 ⅓ cup rolled oats
4 eggs
1 ⅓ cup Greek yogurt (I like Fage 2%, see page 146)
1 teaspoon vanilla
3 teaspoons lemon extract
4 teaspoons baking powder
4 teaspoons poppy seeds
Nonstick cooking spray

PREPARATION:
1. Blend all the ingredients (except poppy seeds) together in a blender.
2. Stir in the poppy seeds.
3. Mix well.
4. Turn your waffle maker to medium heat.
5. Spray with nonstick cooking spray.
6. Pour the batter into the waffle maker.
7. Cook them until they're golden brown (just a few minutes).

OATMEAL

SERVINGS: 1 / 1 bowl of oatmeal
PREP TIME: 2 minutes
COOK TIME: 8 minutes

INGREDIENTS:
½ cup water
¼ cup old-fashioned whole-grain rolled oats
1 apple, diced
½ teaspoon cinnamon
½ teaspoon vanilla extract
1 tablespoon nut butter of choice (no sugar added)
Drizzle of raw honey

PREPARATION:
1. Bring the water to a boil in a small saucepan.
2. Add the oats.
3. Reduce the heat to medium, add the cinnamon and vanilla extract, and stir.
4. Add the apple, stir, and turn the heat to low. Let it simmer for 5 minutes.
5. Turn the heat off and stir in the nut butter.
6. Pour it into a small bowl and drizzle it with raw honey.
7. Enjoy.

ROAST BEEF

And goat cheese

SWEET POTATO TOAST
PANINI

3

LUNCHES

Healthy, quick lunches can be tricky, but here are some REALLY tasty options that don't take much time or effort at all! It is important to take care of yourself even when you are super busy. Stopping to enjoy lunch for a few minutes should always be an option!

HEALTHY BACON, LETTUCE, TOMATO, and EGG

SERVINGS: 1 / 1 sandwich
PREP TIME: 5 minutes
COOK TIME: 5 minutes

INGREDIENTS:
Nonstick cooking spray
2 slices sprouted rye bread (or bread of choice; see chapter 12 for my favorite)
1 egg
2 slices cooked turkey bacon (see page 12)
3 slices tomato
½ cup arugula
¼ avocado
2 teaspoons ghee
Himalayan salt, to taste
Freshly ground black pepper, to taste

PREPARATION:
1. Heat a frying pan over medium heat.
2. After a few minutes, spray it with cooking spray.
3. After a few more minutes, crack an egg into the pan and sprinkle it with salt and pepper (in the meantime, while doing steps 1–3, slice your tomato and cut your avocado).
4. Toast your bread.
5. Add turkey bacon to the pan just to heat it.
6. Flip the egg when it's ready (I like mine over medium).
7. When the toast pops, spread ghee on both pieces.
8. Place the arugula, tomato, and avocado (I like to spread mine on one piece of toast) on the toast and sprinkle them with a tiny bit more salt and pepper.
9. Place the bacon and egg on top.
10. Cut it in half, and enjoy every bite!

HEALTHY COBB SALAD

SERVINGS: 1 / 1 individual salad
PREP TIME: 10 minutes
COOK TIME: Nada (as long as you already have cooked turkey bacon and eggs on hand)

INGREDIENTS:
1 cup chopped romaine lettuce
½ cup baby spinach
1 small tomato, chopped
1 hard-boiled egg, cut into quarters (see page 14)
2 slices cooked turkey bacon, chopped (see page 12)
2 tablespoons blue cheese
¼ avocado, chopped
2–3 tablespoons of salad dressing of choice (my favorite on this salad is Tessemae's Lemon Garlic; see chapter 12)

PREPARATION:
1. Place the lettuce, spinach, and tomato in a salad bowl.
2. Top it with the egg, bacon, blue cheese, and avocado.
3. Drizzle the dressing over the top and enjoy!

**I also make this salad with fried eggs if I don't have hardboiled eggs on hand.

TUNA SALAD

SERVINGS: 1
PREP TIME: 15 minutes
COOK TIME: Nada

INGREDIENTS:
1 5-ounce can chunk light tuna, packed in water, drained
1 teaspoon Primal Kitchen Mayo (see chapter 12)
½ tablespoon Dijon mustard
½ medium red bell pepper, chopped
1 tablespoon fresh tarragon, chopped

PREPARATION:
1. Combine all the ingredients in a bowl and mix them well.
2. Serve the mixture inside a tomato (with the insides scooped out), over a salad, or on bread of your choice.

EGG SALAD

SERVINGS: 1 / 1 sandwich
PREP TIME: 5 minutes
COOK TIME: Nada

INGREDIENTS:
2 hard-boiled eggs (hopefully, you prepped them for the week; see page 14)
1 tablespoon Primal Kitchen Mayo (see chapter 12)
1 dash Himalayan salt
1 sprinkle freshly ground black pepper
1 green onion, chopped
2 slices potato toast (see page 11), or you could use sprouted rye bread or any bread of choice
1 dash of Everything but the Bagel seasoning (see chapter 12)

PREPARATION:
1. Mash the eggs in a bowl.
2. Add the Primal Kitchen Mayo and mix well.
3. Add some salt and pepper and stir.
4. Place the egg salad on the bread.
5. Dash some Everything but the Bagel seasoning and sprinkle the green onions on top.
6. Serve!

QUESADILLA

SERVINGS: 1
PREP TIME: 5 minutes
COOK TIME: 5 minutes

INGREDIENTS:
1 corn tortilla
3 tablespoons cheddar cheese
¼ avocado
1 tablespoon Greek yogurt (I like Fage 2%, see page 146)
 1 dash Himalayan salt
1 sprinkle freshly ground black pepper
1 tablespoon cilantro

PREPARATION:
1. Place the tortilla on a plate.
2. Cover half with the cheese.
3. Fold it closed and place it in a panini press (or a George Foreman like I do).
4. THAT'S IT!!!
5. Spread the Greek yogurt on top.
6. Add the avocado—I like to smash mine and spread it.
7. Top it with a dash of salt and pepper and the cilantro . . . DELISH!

GRILLED CHEESE

SERVINGS: 1/ 1 sandwich
PREP TIME: 5 minutes
COOK TIME: 6 minutes

INGREDIENTS:
2 teaspoons ghee
2 slices rye sprouted bread (or bread of choice; see chapter 12 for my favorite)
2 slices turkey bacon, each cut in half (see page 12)
2-3 slices cheddar cheese
2–3 slices tomato
¼ cup arugula

PREPARATION:
1. Melt the ghee in a nonstick skillet over medium heat.
2. Place the cheese, bacon, tomato, and arugula on one slice of bread and top it with the other slice.
3. Add the sandwich to the skillet and cover it. Cook 2–3 minutes until golden brown.
4. Flip it and cook the other side.
5. Place it on a plate, cut it in half, and serve it warm!

roast beef flatbread panini

ROAST BEEF FLATBREAD PANINI

SERVINGS: 1 / 1 sandwich
PREP TIME: 5 minutes
COOK TIME: 4 minutes

INGREDIENTS:

1 Flatout Flatbread or sweet potato toast (or bread of choice; see chapter 12 for

flatbreads)

6 slices roast beef (I love Boar's Head)

4 roasted red peppers (from a jar)

4 cups goat cheese (I prefer semisoft for this recipe)

PREPARATION:
1. Place the roast beef on the bread.
2. Place the red peppers on top.
3. Top the red peppers with the goat cheese.
4. Press it in a panini maker (secret . . . I use a George Foreman ;)).

**Switch up the toppings for a variety . . . maybe arugula and tomato one day?? Like most of my recipes, the options are endless! Have fun with them!

GROWN-UP PB&J

SERVINGS: 1 / 1 sandwich
PREP TIME: 5 minutes
COOK TIME: Nada

INGREDIENTS:
1 Flatout Foldit Flatbread or 2 slices bread of your choice (see chapter 12 for my favorites)
2 teaspoons nut butter of your choice (no sugar added)
5 smashed fresh strawberries (or skip the strawberries and use 1 tablespoon spreadable fruit)

PREPARATION:
1. Place the flatbread open on a plate.
2. Spread the nut butter on one side of the flatbread.
3. Spread the smashed strawberries on top.
4. Fold and enjoy!

4
DINNERS

These are some of my family's favorite dinners. Don't look too much into the time they take; they are all pretty simple, and you will find your groove with cooking them. The best part is they are delicious, and you will look forward to eating a healthy dinner—at least I do, LOL!

NO MESS SALMON FAJITAS

SERVINGS: 4
PREP TIME: 30 to marinade salmon / 15 minutes of prep while salmon marinades
COOK TIME: 20 minutes

INGREDIENTS:
4 5-ounce salmon fillets
3 bell peppers (any color), sliced
1 large white onion, sliced
3 tablespoons homemade taco seasoning (see page 138)
1 tablespoon oil (avocado or coconut)
4 tablespoons cilantro
4 ounces queso fresco, crumbled

MARINADE:
2 tablespoons oil (avocado or coconut)
3 tablespoons fresh lime juice
2 tablespoons coconut amino, liquid amino, or low-sodium soy sauce
2 fresh garlic cloves, chopped

PREPARATION:
1. Make the marinade by . . .
   Whisking together all the marinade ingredients in a large bowl. Reserve 1 tablespoon to use later for the veggies.
2. Add the salmon to the marinade bowl. Let it sit at room temperature for 30 minutes. Meanwhile, prep the veggies . . . .
3. Preheat the oven to 400 degrees. Line a baking sheet with foil.
4. Add the sliced onion and bell peppers to the baking sheet.
5. Sprinkle them with the tablespoon of taco seasoning, tablespoon of oil, and reserved tablespoon of the marinade. Toss until they are evenly coated and spread them evenly on the baking sheet.
6. Place the salmon on top of the veggies and rub it with the remaining taco seasoning.

7. Bake them for about 20 minutes.

8. Remove them from the oven and place them on plates (maybe with a side of quinoa, brown rice, or the Southwest black bean salad on page 106).

9. Sprinkle everything with queso fresco and cilantro.

10. Enjoy every bite and . . . NO CLEANUP!

SKINNY BEEF PICADILLO

SERVINGS: 4
PREP TIME: 15 minutes
COOK TIME: 15–20 minutes

INGREDIENTS:
1 tablespoon olive oil
4 garlic cloves, chopped
½ medium yellow onion, chopped
1 green bell pepper, diced
1 red bell pepper, diced
1 pound lean ground beef
½ teaspoon black pepper
½ teaspoon Himalayan salt
1 8-ounce can tomato sauce (no salt or added sugar)
2 bay leaves
½ teaspoon garlic salt
1 teaspoon cumin
¼ cup stuffed pimento olives (cut in half)

PREPARATION:
1. In a large pan, heat the oil and add the onion and garlic. Cook for 2–3 minutes.
2. Add the red and green peppers, and cook for about 5 minutes.
3. Add the ground beef, salt, and pepper and cook until the meat is no longer pink.
4. Strain the oils/fat and discard, return the mixture to the pan.
5. Add the tomato sauce, bay leaves, garlic salt, and cumin.
6. Add the olives, stir, and cook the mixture for another few minutes.
7. Reduce the heat to low and simmer until you are ready to serve.
8. I like to serve mine over spaghetti squash and quinoa mixed together (my kids like this over yellow rice).

ONE POT SPIRALIZED ZUCCHINI SHRIMP SCAMPI

SERVINGS: 4
PREP TIME: 15–20 minutes
COOK TIME: 15 minutes

INGREDIENTS:
4 tablespoons olive oil
6 cloves garlic, chopped
1 teaspoon red pepper flakes (you may want to leave this out, or reduce it for the kiddos)
2 pounds shrimp, peeled and deveined
4 tablespoons freshly squeezed lemon juice
1 teaspoon fresh lemon zest
1 teaspoon Himalayan salt
½ teaspoon freshly ground black pepper
6 medium-sized zucchinis, spiralized
4 tablespoons grated parmesan cheese
4 tablespoons fresh parsley, chopped

PREPARATION:
1. Heat a large skillet over medium-high heat, and add the oil.
2. Add the garlic to the oil and cook for 2 minutes, stirring a few times.
3. Add the shrimp, salt, pepper, and red pepper flakes to the hot oil and garlic. Cook, stirring occasionally, until the shrimp is pink and cooked through—about 4–5 minutes.
4. Add the lemon juice and lemon zest.
5. Add the spiralized zucchini noodles and parmesan and toss until well combined—about 1–2 minutes.
6. Garnish it with parsley.
7. What's better than only one pot to clean?!?!

PARMESAN MEATBALLS

SERVINGS: 4
PREP TIME: 10–15 minutes
COOK TIME: 20–25 minutes

INGREDIENTS:
Nonstick cooking spray
1 pound lean ground turkey
½ yellow onion, chopped
5 cloves garlic, chopped
1 egg
½ cup whole grain bread crumbs
2 tablespoon fresh Italian parsley, chopped and divided (one for topping once done)
1 cup freshly grated parmesan cheese
1 teaspoon Himalayan salt
1 teaspoon freshly ground black pepper

PREPARATION:
1. Preheat the oven to 400 degrees.
2. Spray a muffin tray/cupcake pan well with nonstick cooking spray.
3. Mix all the ingredients (with your hands) until they're thoroughly combined.
4. Roll the mixture into 12 balls and place one in each muffin/cupcake cup.
5. Spray the tops with nonstick cooking spray.
6. Bake for 30–35 minutes or until they're browned and cooked throughout, flipping them halfway through.
7. Top them with a little parsley and serve (I love mine with cauliflower rice)!

STEAK FAJITAS

SERVINGS: 4 / 2 fajitas each
PREP TIME: 10–15 minutes
COOK TIME: 25 minutes

INGREDIENTS:

1 tablespoon olive oil

3 medium bell peppers (any color), cut into strips

1 medium yellow onion, sliced

4 cloves garlic, finely chopped

1 pound extra-lean beef sirloin, cut into 2-inch strips

2 ½ teaspoons taco seasoning (see page 138)

1 teaspoon crushed red pepper flakes

½ cup fresh salsa (store bought or homemade)

8 6-inch corn tortillas, warm

4 tablespoons plain Greek yogurt (see chapter 12 for my favorite)

½ cup chopped fresh cilantro

1 lime, cut into wedges

Preparation:

1. Heat the oil in a large nonstick skillet over medium-high heat.

2. Add the bell peppers and onion and cook, stirring occasionally, for 5 to 6 minutes or until the onion is translucent and the peppers are tender.

3. Add the garlic, and stir frequently for 1 minute.

4. Add the beef and cook until the meat is no longer pink.

5. Add the taco seasoning and red pepper flakes and cook for 5–7 minutes.

5. Add the salsa and cook, stirring frequently for 2 to 3 minutes or until heated through.

6. Evenly top each tortilla with the beef mixture, yogurt, cilantro, and a squeeze of lime juice.

DINNER IS PREPPED!

66

SOUTHWEST CILANTRO MINI TURKEY BURGERS

SERVINGS: 4 / 2 burgers each (8 total)
PREP TIME: 10–15 minutes
COOK TIME: 15 minutes

INGREDIENTS:
1 pound lean ground turkey
½ cup black beans
½ cup corn
1 teaspoon Himalayan salt
½ teaspoon freshly ground black pepper
1 cup of cilantro, chopped, divided between cooking and serving
Nonstick cooking spray
4 tablespoons Greek yogurt (I like Fage 2%, see page 146)
Buns of choice, if desired (we do not eat them on buns)

PREPARATION:
1. In a large mixing bowl, combine the ground turkey, corn and beans (both strained and rinsed if they're from a can), salt, pepper, and cilantro (all but about 2 tablespoons).
2. Mix all the ingredients (with your hands) until they're thoroughly combined.
3. Form 8 burger patties.
4. Heat a nonstick skillet over medium-high heat and spray it with cooking spray.
5. Add the burgers to the skillet and cover.
6. Cook them for 10 minutes or until they're fully cooked. Flip halfway through.
7. Place them on plates and spread Greek yogurt on top.
8. Sprinkle them with a little cilantro, and voila! My kiddos like theirs with white jasmine rice. My hubby and I like ours with cilantro lime cauliflower rice (see side dishes, page 108).

MARINATED VEGGIES WITH ORGANIC CHICKEN SAUSAGE

SERVINGS: 4
PREP TIME: 15 minutes + 30 minutes to marinate veggies
COOK TIME: 20 minutes

INGREDIENTS:

2 teaspoons avocado or olive oil

2 tablespoons balsamic vinegar

2 tablespoons fresh lime juice

2 cloves garlic, chopped

1 dash Himalayan salt

1 sprinkle freshly ground black pepper

1 pound green beans, ends removed

2 medium zucchinis, sliced

2 medium summer (crookneck) squash, sliced

1 cup cherry tomatoes, halved

1 medium bell pepper (any color), sliced

1 medium red onion, sliced

4 cooked all-natural chicken sausage (that does not have preservatives and is not high in sodium), sliced

2 tablespoons basil, chopped

PREPARATION:

1. To make the marinade, combine the oil, vinegar, lime juice, and garlic in a medium bowl and whisk to blend.

2. Sprinkle in salt and pepper and whisk it again. Set the marinade aside.

3. Place the green beans, zucchini, summer squash, tomatoes, bell pepper, and onion in a resealable plastic bag (or large bowl). Add the marinade, close the bag, and shake to

blend.

4. Let the veggies marinate for 30 minutes.

5. Preheat the oven to 400 degrees.

6. Place the veggie mixture on a large baking sheet lined with foil.

7. Add the sausage and spread it out evenly.

8. Bake it for 20 minutes, turning occasionally, until the vegetables begin to soften.

9. Sprinkle it with basil before serving.

HEALTHY INSTANT POT SHEPHERD'S PIE

SERVINGS: 6
PREP TIME: 10 minutes
COOK TIME: 15–20 minutes

INGREDIENTS:
2 tablespoons tomato paste
¼ cup water
1 small yellow onion, chopped
8 ounces frozen veggies of choice (I like mixed veggies that have peas and carrots)
½ teaspoon Himalayan salt
¼ teaspoon freshly ground black pepper
¼ teaspoon dried thyme
1 pound lean ground turkey
2 tablespoons Worcestershire sauce
2 20-ounce packages of frozen mashed cauliflower
2 teaspoons onion salt (I like Trader Joe's)

PREPARATION:
1. In an electric pressure cooker, whisk the tomato paste and water together.
2. Stir in the onion, frozen veggies (except the mashed cauliflower), salt, pepper, and thyme.
3. Top it with ground turkey and Worcestershire sauce.
4. Seal the cooker and cook it on manual for 8 minutes.
5. Carefully quick-release the steam.
6. Heat the oven broiler to high.
7. Cook the mashed cauliflower in the microwave.
8. Stir the onion salt into the mashed cauliflower.

9. Break up the cooked ground turkey and stir in 1.5 cups of mashed cauliflower to thicken the sauce.
10. Transfer to a 1-quart soufflé dish.
11. Top the ground turkey mixture with the remaining mashed cauliflower.
12. Broil it until it's browned (3–5 minutes).
13. Scoop it and serve!

GREEK SPAGHETTI SQUASH TOSS

SERVINGS: 4
PREP TIME: 15 minutes
COOK TIME: 20 minutes (if the squash is already prepped) / 50 minutes (if you're baking the squash)

INGREDIENTS:

2 teaspoons olive oil

½ cup red onion, thinly sliced

2 garlic cloves, chopped

2/3 cup unsalted chickpeas, rinsed and drained

1 teaspoon chopped fresh thyme

12 cherry tomatoes, halved

3 cups **COOKED** spaghetti squash (see pages 15–16; this must be made at least an hour in advance)

2 cups baby spinach, torn

1 dash Himalayan salt

4 tablespoons crumbled feta cheese

PREPARATION:

1. Heat the oil in medium skillet over medium-high heat.
2. Add the onion and garlic and cook for about 4 minutes.
3. Add the chickpeas, thyme, and tomatoes and cook for 1 minute.
4. Add the spaghetti squash, spinach, and salt and toss gently to combine. Cook for 2 more minutes or until spinach is wilted.
5. Sprinkle it with cheese.
6. Serve it . . . I like to top mine with chicken (grilled, baked, or even rotisserie) or shrimp.

CRUSTED COCONUT CHICKEN

SERVINGS: 4
PREP TIME: 10 minutes
COOK TIME: 20 minutes

INGREDIENTS:

2 boneless, skinless chicken breasts, filleted to make 4 pieces of chicken
2 tablespoons olive oil
1 cup unsweetened coconut flakes
4 dashes Himalayan salt
4 sprinkles freshly ground black pepper

PREPARATION:

1. Preheat the oven to 350 degrees.
2. Line a baking sheet with foil.
3. Trim and cut the chicken breasts.
4. Rub olive oil on the chicken.
5. Dip the oil-coated chicken in coconut flakes (you may need to pat the coconut on to make sure it stays).
6. Place the chicken on the lined baking sheet.
7. Dash/sprinkle salt and pepper on top of each piece.
8. Bake them for 20 minutes.
9. Serve them with whatever sides you're in the mood for . . . definitely a veggie!

TURKEY BOLOGNESE SPAGHETTI SQUASH

SERVINGS: 4

PREP TIME: 10 minutes

COOK TIME: 45 minutes (if baking the squash) / 15–20 minutes (if you only have to make the Bolognese)

INGREDIENTS:

2 spaghetti squashes

1 2/3 tablespoons olive oil (2/3 tablespoon for squash)

1 onion, chopped

4 cloves garlic, chopped

1 pound lean ground turkey

1 ¾ cups diced tomatoes

1 teaspoon chili flakes

3 ½ teaspoon Himalayan salt (2 teaspoons for squash)

2 teaspoons freshly ground black pepper (1 teaspoon for squash)

1 teaspoon dried thyme

1 teaspoon Italian seasoning

Marinara sauce (no sugar added) of choice

1 tablespoon fresh Italian parsley, chopped

Parmesan cheese for serving, grated or shredded

PREPARATION:

1. Preheat the oven to 400 degrees.
2. Cut the spaghetti squash in half lengthwise.
3. Scoop all seeds out using a fork.
4. Rub a teaspoon of olive oil, ½ teaspoon salt, and ¼ teaspoon pepper on each half of the spaghetti squash.
5. Place the squash face down on a foil-lined baking sheet.
6. Bake it for 40 minutes.

7. In a large pan, heat the remaining oil and add the onion and garlic. Cook them for about 3 minutes.
8. Add the ground turkey and cook until it's no longer pink.
9. Strain the oils/fat and return the mixture to the pan.
10. Season it with chili flakes, salt, pepper, thyme, and Italian seasoning.
11. Add the tomatoes and stir.
12. Pour the marinara sauce in the pan and bring it to a boil.
13. Reduce the heat to low and simmer it until you are ready to serve.
14. Remove the squash from the oven and use a fork to scoop the insides out (once it's cooled enough to handle).
15. Serve the Bolognese sauce over the spaghetti squash (you could serve it over a favorite whole-wheat pasta or zoodles, too . . . these are different options for the kiddos).
16. Sprinkle it with fresh parsley and some parmesan cheese.

BE CREATIVE WITH YOUR PIZZA TOPPINGS . . . HAVE FUN WITH IT!

5

GUILTLESS PIZZAS

Who doesn't want to enjoy pizza?!?!?! Here are some awesome options that I can honestly say taste better than most pizzas. They are all healthy options AND . . . you will not feel guilty after enjoying EVERY bite!

BBQ CHICKEN FLATBREAD

SERVINGS: 6 / 6 individual flatbreads
**You do not have to make 6. Make as few as you like and save the rest of the ingredients for another day/recipe, OR make them all and have leftovers. They are actually GREAT as leftovers!
PREP TIME: 10 minutes
COOK TIME: 8–10 minutes + 3–4 hours to cook the chicken (which should be prepared in advance; see page 13)

INGREDIENTS:
Package of 6 flatbread pizza crusts (I like Flatout Flatbread) OR my homemade cauliflower crust (pages 83-84).
9 teaspoons + 4 splashes BBQ Sauce (I like G Hughes Smokehouse Sugar Free Honey BBQ Sauce) (9 teaspoons for the pizza + 4 splashes for the chicken)
1 pound boneless, skinless chicken thighs (this recipe is also in food prep on page 13)
8 ounces semisoft goat cheese
4 ounces crumbled goat cheese
8 ounces extra-sharp cheddar cheese, shredded
2 hearty bunches cilantro
¼ large red onion, chopped

PREPARATION:
1. Make the shredded chicken in the crockpot if you didn't already prep it for the week (see page 13).
    - Put the chicken in the crockpot.
    - Put 2 healthy splashes of BBQ sauce on the chicken.
    - Set the crockpot to low and cook for 3–4 hours (until the chicken can be shredded with a fork).
    - Shred the chicken.
    - Strain the juices from chicken, put the chicken back in the crockpot, and add a few more splashes of BBQ sauce.

WHEN YOU ARE READY TO MAKE AND SERVE THE PIZZAS . . .
2. Preheat the oven to 400 degrees.

3. Line your baking sheets with foil and lay out the pizza crusts.
4. Spread about 1 ½ teaspoons of BBQ sauce on each flatbread.
5. Put some of the semisoft goat cheese on top of the BBQ sauce.
6. Add chicken to the flatbread.
7. Top the chicken with lots of cilantro (#cilantrolover), a little bit of red onion (however you like it), some cheddar cheese, and a little sprinkle of crumbled goat cheese.
8. Bake them until the cheese melts, about 8–10 minutes.
9. Top them with another little sprinkle of cilantro.
10. ENJOY!

MEXICAN FLATBREAD PIZZA

SERVINGS: 6 / 6 individual flatbreads
**You do not have to make 6. Make as few as you like and save the rest of the ingredients for another day/recipe, OR make them all and have leftovers. They are actually GREAT as leftovers!

PREP TIME: 10 minutes
COOK TIME: 8–10 minutes + 3–4 hours to cook the chicken (which should be prepared in advance; see page 13)

INGREDIENTS:
Package of 6 flatbread pizza crusts (I like Flatout Flatbread) OR my homemade cauliflower crust (pages 83-84).
½ cup + 6 teaspoons salsa verde (I like Trader Joe's) (½ cup for the chicken and 6 teaspoons for the pizzas)
1 pound boneless, skinless chicken breasts (the recipe is also in food prep on page 13)
1 can refried beans
8 ounces shredded Mexican cheese
8 ounces queso fresco, crumbled
2 hearty bunches cilantro
¼ large yellow onion, chopped

PREPARATION:
1. Make the shredded chicken in the crockpot if you didn't already prep it for the week (see page 13).
    ▢ Put the chicken in the crockpot.
    ▢ Pour ½ cup of salsa verde on the chicken.
    ▢ Set the crockpot to low and cook for 3–4 hours (until the chicken can be shredded with a fork).
    ▢ Shred the chicken.

WHEN YOU ARE READY TO MAKE AND SERVE THE PIZZAS . . .
2. Preheat the oven to 400 degrees.
3. Line your baking sheets with foil and lay out the pizza crusts.
4. Spread about 1 tablespoon of refried beans on each flatbread.

5. Top the beans with a teaspoon of salsa verde.

6. Add some chicken to each flatbread.

7. Put some Mexican cheese over the chicken.

8. Top them with lots of cilantro (#cilantrolover), a little bit of yellow onion (however you like it), and some queso fresco.

9. Bake them until the cheese melts, about 8–10 minutes.

10. Top them with another little sprinkle of cilantro.

11. ENJOY!

CAULIFLOWER PIZZA CRUST

SERVINGS: 2 / 2 individual (8-inch crusts)
PREP TIME: 25 minutes
COOK TIME: 15–25 minutes

INGREDIENTS:
Nonstick cooking spray
3 cups fresh cauliflower rice
¼ teaspoon Himalayan salt
½ teaspoon dried basil
½ teaspoon dried oregano
½ teaspoon garlic powder
**optional—a few shakes crushed red pepper
¼ cup parmesan cheese, grated or shredded
¼ cup mozzarella cheese, grated or sheredded
1 egg

PREPARATION:
1. Place a pizza stone in the oven (or a baking sheet if you don't have a pizza stone).
2. Preheat the oven to 450 degrees.
3. On a cutting board, place a large piece of parchment paper and spray it with nonstick cooking spray.
4. Pulse your cauliflower in your food processor for about 30 seconds until it is powdery like snow. You should end up with 2–3 cups of cauliflower "snow."
5. Place the cauliflower in a microwave-safe bowl and cover it. Microwave it for 4 minutes.
6. Dump the cooked cauliflower into a clean tea towel or kitchen towel and allow it to cool for a bit before attempting the next step.
7. Once the cauliflower is cool enough to handle, wrap it in the towel and wring the heck out of it. You want to squeeze out as much water as possible. This will ensure you get a chewy pizza-like crust instead of a crumbly mess.
8. Put the cauliflower into a bowl and add the cheese, salt, basil, oregano, garlic powder, and a dash of red pepper flakes (if you want).
9. Add your egg and mix it with your hands.

10. Use your hands to form the dough into two pizza crusts on your parchment paper. Pat them down thoroughly—you want them tightly formed. Don't make them too thick or too thin.

11. Using a cutting board, slide the parchment paper onto your hot pizza stone or baking sheet in the oven.

12. Bake them for 8–11 minutes until they turn golden brown.

13. Remove them from the oven.

14. Add your toppings (one of the recipes in this cookbook or your own) . . . maybe pesto, goat cheese, turkey bacon, arugula, figs, and pine nuts ????

15. Slide the parchment with the topped pizzas back into the hot oven and cook them for another 5–10 minutes.

** I PROMISE this is not as hard as it sounds . . . you can totally make this, and it is WAY better than any store-bought cauliflower crust—I can promise you that!

FRESH MOZZARELLA PIZZA (perfect for the kiddos)

SERVINGS: 6 / 6 individual flatbreads
PREP TIME: 5 minutes
COOK TIME: 8–10 minutes

INGREDIENTS:
Package of 6 flatbread pizza crusts (I like Flatout Flatbread) OR my homemade cauliflower crust, pages 83-84.
9 teaspoons marinara or pizza sauce (no added sugar) (1 ½ teaspoon for each pizza)
8 ounces freshly sliced mozzarella cheese
8 ounces shredded mozzarella cheese

PREPARATION:
1. Preheat the oven to 400 degrees.
2. Line your baking sheets with foil and lay out the pizza crusts.
3. Spread your sauce on each crust.
4. Add your fresh mozzarella.
   **OPTIONAL . . . add any other toppings of your choice (not in the ingredients list).
5. Top the, with shredded mozzarella.
6. Bake them until the cheese melts, about 8–10 minutes.
7. ENJOY!

6
APPETIZERS

It's always fun to have appetizers! Here are some great healthier options, and again, they are EASY to make.

CAPRESE-STUFFED GARLIC GHEE PORTOBELLO MUSHROOMS

SERVINGS: 5–6 (1 mushroom each)
PREP TIME: 10 minutes
COOK TIME: 8–10 minutes

INGREDIENTS:
GARLIC GHEE:
2 tablespoons ghee
2 cloves garlic, chopped
1 tablespoon freshly chopped parsley
MUSHROOMS:
5–6 Portobello mushrooms, stems removed, washed and dried thoroughly with a paper towel
5–6 fresh mozzarella cheese balls, sliced very thin
1 cup grape (or cherry) tomatoes, sliced thin
1 teaspoon Himalayan salt
½ teaspoon freshly ground black pepper
fresh basil, chopped to garnish
¼ cup balsamic vinegar

PREPARATION:
1. Preheat the oven to the broil setting on high heat.
2. Mix all the garlic ghee ingredients in a small saucepan (or you can do this in the microwave). Melt them until the garlic is fragrant.
3. Brush the bottoms of each mushroom and place them (buttered-side down) on a baking sheet.
4. Brush any remaining garlic ghee over the insides of each cap.
5. Fill each mushroom with the mozzarella and tomatoes.
6. Top them with salt and pepper.
7. Broil them on the top rack of your oven until the cheese has melted and is golden, about 8 minutes.
8. Top them with basil and drizzle them with balsamic vinegar.

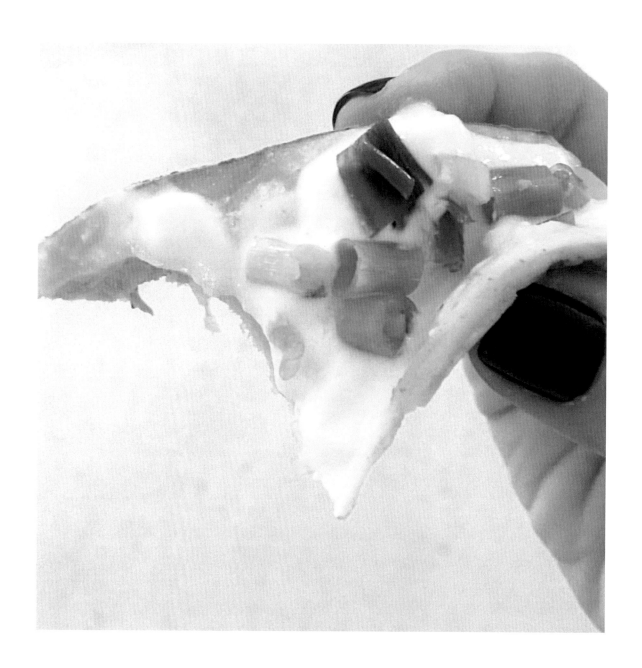

HEALTHY POTATO SKINS

I absolutely LOVE how easy these are to make if you prep the potato toast in advance!! I will have one or two on a random afternoon as a healthy/delicious snack because they take minutes to make when the potato toast is ready to go in the fridge!

SERVINGS: 6/2 potato skins each
PREP TIME: 5 minutes
COOK TIME: 5–10 minutes

INGREDIENTS:

12 slices of potato toast (hopefully, you already prepped them, see page 11)
6 teaspoons ghee
12 teaspoons Greek yogurt (I like Fage 2%, see page 146)
Himalayan salt (just enough to sprinkle on each potato skin)
Freshly ground black pepper (just enough to sprinkle on each potato skin)
1 cup fresh green onions, chopped (you could use dried chives, but use less if you do)

PREPARATION:
1. Heat the potato toast in the toaster or toaster oven (see page 11).
2. Spread ghee on each piece of potato toast (about a half a teaspoon each)
3. Spread the Greek yogurt on top of the ghee (about a teaspoon each).
4. Sprinkle them with salt and pepper.
5. Top them with chives
6. VOILA—THAT IS IT!!!

CHEESE-STUFFED JALAPEÑO PEPPERS

SERVINGS: 5 / 4 peppers each
PREP TIME: 15 minutes
COOK TIME: 10 minutes

INGREDIENTS:
10 jalapeño peppers
6 ounces semisoft goat cheese
6 ounces shredded white sharp cheddar
6 ounces cottage cheese
1/8 teaspoon Himalayan salt
1/8 teaspoon freshly ground black pepper
⅛ teaspoon cumin

PREPARATION:
1. Heat the grill to medium heat.
2. Cut the jalapeño peppers in half.
3. Scoop out the seeds (if you like super spicy, leave the seeds in).
4. Mix all the cheeses together.
5. Add the salt, pepper, and cumin and mix them well.
6. Stuff the cheese in the peppers.
7. Grill them over medium heat for about 10 minutes or until the cheese melts.
8. Serve!

ZUCCHINI CHIPS

SERVINGS: 6
PREP TIME: 15–20 minutes
COOK TIME: 20–30 minutes

INGREDIENTS:
3 large zucchinis, thinly sliced
6 teaspoons olive oil
1 ½ cups unsweetened, shredded coconut flakes
1 teaspoon Himalayan salt
½ teaspoon freshly ground black pepper

PREPARATION:
1. Preheat the oven to 400 degrees.
2. Line a baking sheet with parchment paper (for no mess, though this is not needed).
3. Toss the zucchini slices in olive oil to coat them well.
4. Dip the zucchini slices in coconut flakes (you may need to pat the coconut on to make sure it stays).
5. Place the zucchini chips on the baking sheet lined in parchment paper.
6. Sprinkle them with salt and pepper.
7. Bake them for 20–30 minutes until they're crisp and browned.

THIS IS THE CORN SALAD ON PAGE 102. WE USE MANY OF THESE SIDE DISHES TO TOP
FISH, TACOS, ETC. AGAIN . . . BE CREATIVE WITH YOUR FOOD!

7
SIDE DISHES

Here are some of my family's favorite side dishes! I can honestly say they are all delicious. I always look forward to them when they are on the menu for the week. Most are great to bring along to BBQs or parties too!

CHICKPEA, FETA, and PARSLEY SALAD

SERVINGS: 6
PREP TIME: 15–20 minutes
COOK TIME: 5 minutes (to sauté onion and garlic)

INGREDIENTS:
1 ½ tablespoons olive oil
1 medium red onion, chopped
3 cloves garlic, chopped
2 15.5-ounce cans chickpeas (garbanzo beans), drained and rinsed
4 green onions, chopped
1 cup parsley, chopped
Juice of 1 lemon
5 ounces feta cheese
1 ½ teaspoons Himalayan salt
1 teaspoon freshly ground black pepper

PREPARATION:

1. Heat 1 tablespoon of the olive oil in a skillet over medium heat. Cook the red onion until it is lightly golden, add the garlic, and cook it until garlic is fragrant. Set it aside to cool.
2. Place the drained and rinsed chickpeas in a salad bowl.
3. Add the feta, scallions, parsley, lemon juice, salt, and pepper.
4. Add the cooled onion and garlic mixture and the remaining oil. Mix it well.
5. Serve!

**This refrigerates well to have on hand and enjoy throughout the week!

CORN SALAD WITH HONEY LIME DRESSING

SERVINGS: 6
PREP TIME: 15–20 minutes
COOK TIME: Nada, unless you are making fresh-cooked corn

INGREDIENTS:
2 15.25-ounce cans of corn (strained) or fresh-cooked corn cut from the cob . . . you could also do cans of roasted corn. We make it all 3 ways in our house!
1 red bell pepper, chopped
1 cucumber, peeled (if you choose—we do both ways), gutted and chopped
⅓ cup red onion, chopped
2 jalapeños, gutted and chopped (optional but recommended for the adults)
1 hearty bunch of cilantro, chopped

FOR DRESSING:
¼ cup olive oil
Juice of 2 limes
2 tablespoons apple cider vinegar
2 tablespoons raw honey
Himalayan salt, to taste
Freshly ground black pepper, to taste
2 avocados, diced (you could make it without avocado and it's still delicious)

PREPARATION:
1. Pour the corn into a large mixing bowl.
2. Add the red pepper, cucumber, red onion, jalapeños (if you want a little kick—we sometimes add them after we've scooped the kiddos' servings out), and cilantro.
3. Prepare the dressing. In a small bowl, add the olive oil, lime juice, apple cider vinegar, raw honey, Himalayan salt, and freshly ground black pepper (to taste). Mix them well.
4. Pour the dressing over the ingredients in the large mixing bowl and stir.
5. Add the avocado and give it a quick stir.
6. VOLIA . . . time to ENJOY!

KALE and BRUSSELS SPROUT SALAD

SERVINGS: 6
PREP TIME: 15–20 minutes
COOK TIME: Nada

INGREDIENTS:
DRESSING:
Juice of 1 lemon
1 tablespoon Dijon mustard
1 teaspoon shallots, chopped
1 clove garlic, chopped
¼ teaspoon Himalayan salt
⅛ teaspoon freshly ground black pepper
¼ cup olive oil
SALAD:
2–3 cups kale, chopped
1 12-ounce bag shredded Brussels sprouts
3–4 slices cooked turkey bacon (see page 12), chopped
¼ cup sliced almonds
½ cup parmesan cheese, shredded

PREPARATION:
1. Mix all the dressing ingredients in a small bowl (except the oil).
2. Whisk in the oil.
3. Mix the kale and Brussels sprouts in a large salad bowl.
4. Throw in the bacon, almonds, and cheese and pour the dressing over the top.
5. Toss them until all the ingredients are evenly distributed.
6. Serve!

SOUTHWEST BLACK BEAN SALAD

SERVINGS: 6
PREP TIME: 15–20 minutes + 30 minutes to marinate in the refrigerator
COOK TIME: Nada

INGREDIENTS:
1 15.5-ounce can black beans, rinsed and drained
9 ounces cooked corn, fresh or frozen (thawed if frozen)
1 medium tomato, chopped
¼ cup red onion, chopped
4 scallions, chopped
1 jalapeño, seeds scooped out and chopped
Juice of 2 limes
1 teaspoon Himalayan salt
½ teaspoon freshly ground black pepper
1 tablespoon olive oil
¼ cup cilantro, chopped
1 avocado, diced

PREPARATION:
1. In a large bowl, combine the beans, corn, tomato, onion, scallions, jalapeño, cilantro, salt, and pepper.
2. Squeeze fresh lime juice over the top and stir in the olive oil.
3. Marinate it in the refrigerator for 30 minutes.
4. Add the avocado just before serving.
5. That is all! It's quick, easy, and delicious!

CILANTRO LIME CAULIFLOWER RICE

SERVINGS: 4
PREP TIME: 15–20 minutes
COOK TIME: 15 minutes

INGREDIENTS:
1 12-ounce bag fresh cauliflower rice
4 tablespoons avocado (or olive) oil
3 cloves garlic, chopped
½ large yellow onion, chopped
½ cup cilantro, chopped + a sprinkle for serving
1 tablespoon white vinegar
Juice of 1 lime
½ teaspoon cumin
½ teaspoon Himalayan salt

PREPARATION:
1. Place the cauliflower rice in food processor for about 30 seconds (or blender) and pulse until it is more of a "snow."
2. Heat 1 tablespoon of oil in a large skillet over medium heat.
3. Sauté the onion and 2 cloves of garlic for 3–4 minutes or until fragrant.
4. Add the cauliflower rice and continue to sauté.
5. Meanwhile, make your sauce. Place the cilantro, vinegar, remaining garlic, lime juice, cumin, and salt in the food processor or blender.
6. While the motor is running, add the remaining oil. Blend until it's smooth.
7. Pour the sauce on top of cauliflower rice, mixing until it's evenly distributed.
8. Remove it from the heat, sprinkle it with cilantro, and serve.

AVOCADO LIME SLAW

SERVINGS: 4
PREP TIME: 10 minutes
COOK TIME: Nada

INGREDIENTS:
10 ounces angel-hair coleslaw (finely shredded green cabbage)
4 scallions, chopped
Juice of 2 limes
¼ teaspoon Himalayan salt
¼ teaspoon freshly ground black pepper
2 avocados, cubed
¼ cup cilantro, chopped (if desired—you can leave it off too)

PREPARATION:
1. Place the coleslaw and green onion in a large mixing bowl.
2. Squeeze the lime juice over the top.
3. Add the salt and pepper and mix well (and the cilantro, if you decide to add it).
4. Add the avocado and toss lightly.
5. Voila—fastest side dish ever!

PEANUT BUTTER NICE CREAM (PAGE 114)

8

8
DESSERTS

OK—we all want to indulge in desserts sometimes! The best part about these recipes is you feel like you're indulging but . . . YOU'RE NOT! They are healthy, so once again, no guilt!

PEANUT BUTTER NICE CREAM

PREP TIME: 5 minutes
COOK TIME: Nada

INGREDIENTS:

2 frozen bananas (cut into slices before freezing)

2 tablespoons nut butter of your choice (no sugar added)

2 splashes unsweetened almond or coconut milk (add until desired consistency)

2 sprinkles cocoa nibs (optional)

2 sprinkles nuts of your choice (optional)

PREPARATION:

1. Blend (sometimes, I even use my NutriBullet for an easier cleanup) the bananas, nut butter, and milk until it is your desired consistency (you could eat it right away or put it in the freezer to make it even more like ice cream . . . you could even double or triple the recipe and keep it in the freezer to pull out when you have an ice-cream craving).
2. Divide it into 2 bowls and sprinkle some cocoa nibs and nuts on top.
3. PERFECTION with no guilt!

VEGAN PEANUT BUTTER COOKIES

SERVINGS: 7–8 / 1 cookie per serving
PREPTIME: 10 minutes + 1 hour of fridge time (if you want soft cookies)
COOK TIME: 8 minutes

INGREDIENTS:

½ cup peanut butter or allergy-friendly sub (no sugar added, if possible)

¾ teaspoon baking soda

3 tablespoons flour (I used 1 of whole wheat and 2 of almond flour, but they all work)

1/3 cup coconut sugar

2 tablespoons unsweetened applesauce

½ teaspoon pure vanilla extract

1/8 teaspoon Himalayan salt

PREPARATION:

1. Preheat the oven to 350 degrees.
2. Combine the dry ingredients in a mixing bowl.
3. Add all the remaining ingredients to the mixing bowl (if your peanut butter is not stirrable, gently warm it to soften) and stir to form a dough.
4. Roll the dough into cookie balls.
5. If you want soft cookies, refrigerate the dough for at least an hour (you can also freeze the balls to bake another time, if you wish).
6. Place the cookies on a nonstick cookie sheet and bake them for 8 minutes. The cookies will look quite underdone when you take them out.
7. Let them cool for at least 10 minutes before removing them from the tray; they firm up while cooling.

HEALTHY PEANUT BUTTER SWIRL BROWNIES

SERVINGS: 9–12 brownies
PREP TIME: 20 minutes
COOK TIME: 15 minutes to bake + refrigerate overnight (if you want them sweet!)

INGREDIENTS:
Nonstick cooking spray

1 15.5-ounce can black beans

2 tablespoons cocoa powder

½ cup rolled oats (I use whole grain)

¼ teaspoon Himalayan salt

1/3 cup raw honey

¼ cup coconut oil

2 teaspoons pure vanilla extract

½ teaspoon baking powder

½ to 2/3 cups chocolate chips

¼ cup nut butter of choice

PREPARATION:

1. Preheat the oven to 350 degrees.
2. Spray an 8 x 8-inch pan with cooking spray.
3. Drain and rinse the beans very well, and pat them dry.
4. Combine all the ingredients (except the chocolate chips and nut butter) in a food processor and blend until they're completely smooth (really blend well).
5. Place the batter in a mixing bowl and stir in the chips.
6. Pour the batter into the greased pan.
7. Gently warm the nut butter until it is easily stirrable, and then drop dollops onto the batter and swirl them with a spoon. You can also sprinkle some chocolate chips on top for presentation.

8. Bake them on the center rack for 15 minutes.

9. Let the still-undercooked brownies cool for 10 minutes, and then refrigerate them overnight. They firm up considerably and taste much sweeter and richer!

PAN-FRIED BANANAS

SERVINGS: 4 / ½ banana each
PREP TIME: 5 minutes
COOK TIME: 5 minutes

INGREDIENTS:
2 bananas, sliced
2 teaspoons ghee
4 teaspoons raw honey
½ teaspoon cinnamon
¼ teaspoon Himalayan salt

PREPARATION:
1. Cook the ghee, honey, cinnamon, and salt in a frying pan over medium heat until bubbling.
2. Place the banana slices in the pan.
3. Once they're browned on one side, flip them.
4. Brown them on other side and VOILA!

CANNOLI CREAM

SERVINGS: 2
PREP TIME: 5 minutes
COOK TIME: Nada

INGREDIENTS:

1 1/3 cups ricotta cheese

2 tablespoons Greek yogurt (I like Fage 2%, see page 146)

2 teaspoons raw honey

1 teaspoon pure vanilla extract

2 sprinkles cocoa nibs (optional)

PREPARATION:

1. Mix the ricotta cheese, Greek yogurt, honey, and vanilla in a bowl.
2. Top it with cocoa nibs.
3. Enjoy every spoonful!

SNACK TIME

9
HEALTHY SNACKS

It was important to me to include these snacks—as simple as they may seem—because sometimes, we overthink! Grabbing a healthy snack does not have to be time consuming or boring. It can be quick and DELICIOUS!

CANDY APPLE SNACK

SERVINGS: 1 apple per person
PREP TIME: 5 minutes
COOK TIME: Nada

INGREDIENTS:
1 apple, sliced thin
2 teaspoons nut butter of choice (no sugar added)
1 teaspoon raw honey
1 sprinkle nuts of choice (optional)
1 sprinkle cocoa nibs (optional)

PREPARATION:
1. Place the apple slices on a plate.
2. Spread the nut butter on top of each slice.
3. Drizzle the raw honey on top.
4. Sprinkle the nuts and cocoa nibs on top if you desire (I recommend both).
5. DELISH!

BANANA TACO SNACK

SERVINGS: 1
PREP TIME: 5 minutes
COOK TIME: Nada

INGREDIENTS:
½ Flatout Flatbread
1 teaspoon nut butter of choice (no sugar added)
½ banana
1 teaspoon raw honey

PREPARATION:
1. Place Flatout Flatbread on a plate.
2. Spread the nut butter on the flatbread.
3. Place half a banana on the nut butter.
4. Drizzle it with raw honey.
5. Wrap the banana like a taco and enjoy!

   **I have this as a pre-run snack a lot.

BANANA SNACK

SERVINGS: 1
PREP TIME: 5 minutes
COOK TIME: Nada

INGREDIENTS:
½ banana
2 teaspoons nut butter of choice (no sugar added)
1 teaspoon raw honey
1 sprinkle nuts of choice (optional)
1 sprinkle cocoa nibs (optional)
1 sprinkle unsweetened coconut flakes (optional)

PREPARATION:
1. Cut the banana in half lengthwise.
2. Top it with nut butter.
3. Drizzle it with raw honey.
4. Sprinkle the nuts, cocoa nibs, and coconut on top, if desired.
5. SWEET CRAVING SATISFIED.

CANDY APPLE YOGURT SNACK

SERVINGS: 1
PREP TIME: 5 minutes
COOK TIME: Nada

INGREDIENTS:
¾ cup Greek yogurt (I like Fage 2%, see page 146)
 1 teaspoon nut butter of choice (no sugar added)
1 apple, cut into cubes
1 teaspoon raw honey
1 sprinkle nuts of choice (optional)

PREPARATION:

1. Mix the yogurt and nut butter together.

2. Mix in the apple pieces.

3. Drizzle it with raw honey.

4. Sprinkle it with nuts.

5. YUM!

10

SALAD DRESSINGS and SEASONINGS

Why not make your own dressing and seasoning when it is this easy?!?!? I am sharing 2 of my favorites!

CILANTRO LIME DRESSING

SERVINGS: 4–6
PREP TIME: 15 minutes
COOK TIME: Nada

INGREDIENTS:
1 hearty bunch of cilantro, leaves pulled off stems (takes a little while, but it's SO WORTH IT)
1 clove garlic
¼ cup avocado oil
¼ cup lime juice
2 teaspoons raw honey

PREPARATION:
1. Another one-step recipe . . . put all the ingredients in the food processor and blend away! It is very important to make sure you don't have stems of the cilantro because they will make the dressing taste bitter.
2. Enjoy this over any salad you like . . . it is my fave over a steak salad!

**Double or triple the recipe to have more on hand in the fridge for the week (I keep mine in a mason jar)!

HOMEMADE TACO SEASONING

TACO SEASONING

SERVINGS: enough for 4 recipes
PREP TIME: 2–5 minutes
COOK TIME: Nada

INGREDIENTS:
¼ cup chili powder
2 tablespoons garlic powder
2 tablespoons onion powder
2 tablespoons cumin
½ tablespoon paprika
⅓ tablespoon Himalayan salt

PREPARATION:
1. ONE STEP . . . simply mix all ingredients together! This makes enough for about 4 recipes—I keep mine in a little mason jar.

11
INNOCENT COCKTAILS

I love a good cocktail from time to time! These two are seriously AMAZING!!! Once you try them, you will never go back!

THE INGREDIENT LINEUP

SKINNY MULE

SERVINGS: 1 drink
PREP TIME: 2–5 minutes

INGREDIENTS:
**I did not provide specific amounts in the ingredient list (they are in the "preparation" of the drink below because you usually always make more than one drink).

Healthier ginger beer (read your ingredients)! My fave is Spectacular Ginger Beer (sweetened with organic agave)
Tito's (just my preference) Vodka

Lime

Mint

PREPARATION:
1. Fill your copper mug (it's all about the glass/cup) with ice.
2. Add 1–2 shots of vodka (I usually do 1.5).
3. Add the ginger beer and a slice of lime (squeeze the juice in).
4. Add some mint leaves!

I LOVE the spice of the Spectacular Ginger Beer!!! ENJOY!

THE INGREDIENT LINEUP

SUPER SKINNY MARGARITA

SERVINGS: 1 drink
PREP TIME: 2 minutes

INGREDIENTS:
**I did not provide specific amounts in the ingredient list (they are in the "preparation" of the drink below because you usually always make more than one drink).

S. Pellegrino Sparkling Water

1800 Coconut Tequila (must be this tequila to get the correct flavoring)

Lime

PREPARATION:
1. Simply fill your glass with ice.
2. Add 1–2 shots of tequila (I usually do 1.5).
3. Add sparkling water.
4. Add lots of freshly squeezed lime juice (maybe a quarter of a lime) and stir!

This sounds so simple and like it can't be anything special . . . trust me, IT IS THE BOMB!!

12
FAVORITE PRODUCTS

These are some of my absolute favorite products. I use them ALL the time.
They appear in many of the recipes in this book. You do not have to use
these specific brands—they are just the brands I prefer. As I mentioned
before, be adventurous with your food! Try new foods, products, brands . . .
I am no way affiliated with these brands.

Made in the USA
Lexington, KY
27 March 2019